Lion's Tooth

Lion's Tooth

Mariegold Heron

SERENDIPITY

First published in 2006 by

Serendipity
First Floor
37 / 39 Victoria Road
Darlington
DL1 5SF

British Library Cataloguing-in-Publication data
A catalogue record for this book is available from the British Library

ISBN 978-1-84394-206 2

Printed and bound by CPI Antony Rowe, Eastbourne

Acknowledgements

A photograph, *Daily Express*
A Quiet Festival, *Poetry Street*
Unruly Garden, *Pennine Platform*
Lion's Tooth, *Poetry Now*
Three Angles of Perception, *Forward Press*
The Jewess, *Poetry Now*
Cloak of Motherhood, *Envoi 125*
I am comforted, *Poetry Monthly*
An Invitation to Mourn, *Voice of a Nation*
Deliverance, *First Time Publications*
Our Housekeeper, *The Key to Life*
Petrarchan Sonnet, *Faith, Hope and Love*
On Wandsworth Bridge, *Poetry Today*
To a Dear Investment Analyst, *Frogmore Papers*
The Waste Tip, *Psychopoetica*
Three short poems, *Still* a short verse journal
Taking to the Bus, displayed within the first fifty of the competition set
    by *Friends of the Earth and Big Wide Words*
Poem-Elegy and accompanying prose, Pringle Award for Art & Poetry
    from *Rethink*

To Theodore and Annie Deppe
Americans in Ireland
full of imaginative advice

and

with thanks for the support of my husband
and of all poetry teachers and friends.

With thanks to Patricia M. Lucey for the cover illustration
and Alex Bage for the colour and design

CONTENTS

TESTIMONIALS FOR MARIEGOLD HERON

Mariegold Heron's poems are deeply felt without ever being sentimental. In a style that is economical and well crafted, she tackles often painful subjects with remarkable honesty. These are courageous poems, sparing neither herself nor the reader.

Carole Satyamurti

Mariegold Heron's poems, published and unpublished, provide a vivid cluster of self portraits, tumbling spontaneously into appetizing mouthfuls of musical verse. About creativity, love, bereavement, life and death; these poems have often forced their way onto paper, shoving aside many of the trivialities of their author's daily life. Passionate feelings alongside sharply observed surroundings a good working recipe for lively personal poetry.

Adeline Hartcup

Mariegold Heron's writing has a striking intensity and an unmistakable style. These combine with her severe restraint to result in poems that are both compelling and memorable.

Maurice Riordan

LION'S TOOTH

The coarse yellow flower
Turns into dandelion clocks
With delicate pappus
Dispersing seeds
Blown by ambivalent
Destiny or chance.

Outside a plain house
I glimpsed a patch
Of blue and yellow.
Bluebells of course,
But the yellow seemed
A cultivated flower.
They were dandelions -
Called an unsightly weed.
I think they're both
Lilies of the field.

EARLY MORNING TEA

Long-married lovers hear a child-blown bird's egg
and live in quiet bliss.
He tries to put a lazy arm
behind her back
while she gulps her honeyed herbal tea.
He lets his arm fall to her side without resentment or regret.

The bedclothes are too thick
and dull the lovers' memory of sharp bereavement.
When a pillow or the quilted counterpane
slips to the floor
the couple feel unnatural cold. Once dressed
they hear no more the child's blown egg –
resignation thinly clothes them.

ELEGY 1966-99

Recalling a CD "Smoke gets in your eyes"
which he played for me and made my spirits rise;
and a dream of his body renewed, I visualize

afternoons on Wimbledon Common;
the bark of silver birch shone in the sun;
I heard talk of everyday and of religion.

Some instinct helped him match his steps to mine.
We loved the ponds and watched the birds in line,
heather or gorse in flower as season's signs.

Hard work to win a second Day School place;
which I thrilled to know he'd gained by steady pace –
hopes raised that illness would efface.

His choice for his walls of Venetian red
or of A. A. Milne's explicit geranium red
and even on dark days a t-shirt tomato red

still seems fresh now he's many months dead;
it brought him no health as the pessimists said. I think it became a
life-affirming red.

COLLECTING FOR MENTAL HEALTH

In the cold and rainy high street
I leant against the wall
Beside a high class grocers
And shook my tin.

A woman wished
She could lend me gloves;
And for my sake
Others deplored the weather.

Students appeared
With stealthy donations.
Young women in elegant coats
Passed by indifferently.
Threadbare men
Gave silver and thanked me
Without my knowing why.

PRESENTS TO PARENTS-IN-LAW

The fallen raindrops on our rose leaves smiled
At the memory of each artless gift:
Plastic flower spray for aborted child.

Pale pink jumper for mother - seeming mild.
It might have been designed a pain to shift.
Some fallen raindrops on our roseleaves smiled.

Print of puppies for guileless father styled,
Chosen his withered hopes to uplift.
Plastic flower spray for a longed for child.

Now mixed loose biscuits in disorder piled
Which create an unending task to sift.
More fallen raindrops on our roseleaves smiled.

By her quiet voice we were beguiled,
Her fine dark hair, white skin - sick love gift:
Plastic flower spray for aborted child.

Though formerly beloved, we're now reviled;
Our role outstayed, we must foresee a rift.
The fallen raindrops on our rose leaves smiled.
Plastic flower spray for aborted child.

TWENTY-FOUR HOUR MEMORIAL

She lit the candle before undressing
feeling pain throughout her body.
The wick burned steadily
within the glass container
casting light on the photo of her son
proudly punting his mother and his dog.

Peter's father removed the candle which
kept him awake; both parents fell asleep.
Next day in the kitchen his mother watched
the light go out and recalled
her post-natal absences and his final jump.

THE YELLOW TEAPOT

I fill it to the brim
but see it empty slowly
now that Peter's dead.

When I call my husband
he says he's scrubbing his shirt.

If I persist with the yellow pot
he finds the tea's grown cold. Too late for talk
I give him the little 'smiley' red and white
and for my second cup endure the chaste and clouded blue.

A BIBLICAL FANTASY

The hairdresser's proprietress,
wearing a thin turquoise robe,
is Mary Magdalene, clever with her fingertips,
able to comfort and incite to laughter.
We greet each other warmly
but her young male assistant
is scheduled for the job.

He's happy with himself
and full of love like St. John;
washes my hair three times;
then as I'm moved from the basin
to sit before the mirror,
wields his tools of heated brush
and flick comb.

The proprietess's husband,
a tall man in a dark suit walks in -
the shop is small and villagelike -
he neither washes his hands
nor passes judgment; he says Good morning
and, as I see in the mirror,
promptly leaves.

AN INVITATION TO MOURN

Our machine washperson
described herself,
when refusing help
with heavy sacks,
as a woman of the nineties.

When Princess Diana died,
Julie crept up to me with tears,
Saying she felt she knew her
and assuming I would share her grief.
In time her child threw flowers.

I had never been familiar with the Royalist press
and Lady Di had been to me a riddle
but admiring how resolute she was
when involved in sensitive issues
and how she touched a leper,
I joined in Julie's sadness.

THE JEWESS

I saw my mother in a dream,
blown up in size
and with a masculine mien -as though
to include her domination.
This Irish house stays firm
surrounded by gale force winds.

I lodge here while studying
and accept Catholic welcome,
but as strong a force as the winds
is more news of Israeli revenge.
(The Beatitudes
grow from Leviticus,

love being known before Christ).
The dream conveyed I should
revere my mother and speak well of her
in spite of her cold expression
She had wit and dignity
and belonged to a suffering race.

LENTEN POEM

Two thousand rabbis were crucified,
Each thinking he was the Messiah,
About the time of Jesus.

I think Jesus would have felt for them
Had he known; perhaps he did.
Like him they belonged to the chosen race.

These men were probably good
Although with hindsight might have been called
Presumptuous or vain.

Jesus drew all men to him
So the quality of his life and teaching
Must have surpassed theirs.

Yet I would in Communion like to remember
All who have kept their integrity
While dying in pain.

IRIS

I noticed yellow flags
Among the elephant leaves
And red branches of dogwood,
But the white belly of a frog
Lying dead on the path
    Arrested my vision.

Next year it seemed they also grew
Higher in the water garden,
Bedded with lush grass and insects
By the American Currant
Which trailed over a disused well:
    I sensed a glory,

And painted a yellow iris
Distinct against undergrowth
Of brown-black washes,
Cherishing the image,
Replanting all uprooted bulbs
    Which might survive.

Now I know that the drier soil
Of the cultivated garden
Breeds clearcut shapes,
More full in flower,
Rich in purples, puce,
    Wine red, pale gold and white.

OUR HOUSEKEEPER

She was a plain woman
Made big by thyroid
But crowned with curly hair.

She loved our neglected son,
Hugged him
And thought him perfect.

When I spoilt her evening out
She sent me flowers ;
When I felt able
To do without her
She gave me
A French book of cookery.

In hospital, dying
She gave me
A bright silk scarf with mimosa.

It was her badge of motherhood.

BOOKS AND MUSIC

Daphne worked quietly in the library
always wearing grey and black,
showing no sign of coquetry.
She was seventeen and

wanted to grow, while keeping still.
When Apollo came and demanded
law and order, she sorted the shelves,
beguiled by the music sheets he carried.

Daphne asked him to play on his lyre
for she knew he was caught with her beauty.
He could not persuade her to transform
a cerebral love into one more earthy.

Impatient, he molested her and she
called on her father, a river god, for help.
He turned her into a shrub -a laurel
with aubergine berries and green shiny leaves.

Standing at the entrance to the library
Daphne now wore colours of her own.
Having spurned carnal love, she shivered.
Apollo called her his favourite tree.

GLOBAL WARNING

The technicolor sky
showed a beauty like Hiroshima.
Earlier poised to cross the road
she'd found the brilliance of the sun
obscured pedestrian red and green.
She took the risk.

Last night's storms
had stripped autumn leaves
in advance and left them floating.
Now the sky turned electric blue,
wind got up again and teased the branches.
She abandoned her shivered umbrella.

Extremes of weather, cold dry patches,
wet weeks with gales, the new day's
pastel streaks and wide screen sunrise
chilled, soaked, lit her up.
Now she longed for acid rain
and the 'Gulf Stream' shifting.

A VERSATILE QUAKER

A Quaker need not believe in God, she says.
Her unrecorded life seems to show it.
She has helped children slow at reading,
played the piano in a pub for cash,
practised music therapy in mental wards -
a constant friend who would not lick your wounds.

For a quiet encounter, she would prefer a place
without sophistication.
She does not bother about dress
and shoots down nice comment.
She reads the Daily Mail for its puzzles
and stays mute about her beliefs.

In a church where she helps with bells
passive lice rest beneath pew carpets.
Ringers jump up and down in the tower,
some transported to the ceiling
by their ropes. Only this Quaker ringer
knows how to stay down to earth.

A Philanthropic Writer

Adeline, passionate, petite,
Author of good prose
About children in great houses,
Life in a Tuscan village,
Or English education,
A versatile reporter;
And teacher of young miscreants.

Now in her seventies, she pecks
At each thought and experience,
Loves plays, exhibits, concerts and films,
Her nice discernment leading her
To refuse invitations
Even when free
And to do so with unashamed grace.

Able to admit a mistake but
Liable to impatience and hasty
Judgments as when sizing up
A shy compere.
She can also offer and withdraw
In an evening her own invitation
To a Seamus Heaney poetry reading.

Eager to help young schizophrenics
To unearth artistic talent,
She'll also spend time to divert
More ordinary troubled souls.
Active herself, clever and quick,
She honours slow thinking and dreams.

A Photograph

Two small boys playing baseball
on the Pacific coast:

The sea is calm,
the sky pale and
slightly flecked with summer clouds,
sand immaculate
though strewn with seaweed
and churned by children's feet.

One boy lifts his bat,
face open with expectation.
The other, in repose, looks down
waiting upon his turn.

I have not known this scene
and yet I feel included.

YOUNGEST CHILD

Grapefruit I'd heard of, held its image close -
round and juicy and bitter -
The aroma covering my brothers.

Our mother, who'd ordered the citrus fruit,
Beckoned me; sent for the sheepskin rug to lie on;

We ate in the open, sucking the yellow pulp -
which for me became an ecstasy -

The nursery now deserted
for one day at least
Breakfast pulley ceased.

Illustration by Eric J. Proctor
Photographed by Simon Heron

NIGHT VISION

I lay awake three hours
and then a square of white
behind the curtains
drew me to the window.
I hoped to see neutral snow -
instead, through the glass,
three moons. Were they
an unbroken family,
Jesus, Mary, Joseph
or the Holy Trinity?
- or lights of my imagination?

DIRGE

Dead leaves dance on the granite pavement.
They ache to draw in sons and daughters.

These are caught in their own wild growing
with love's seduction and love's thick tangles.

They only hear the cogent rhythm
and keep their bodies close.

CHINA

It's too good for you, she said,
about a new china dish
To keep my breakfast warm.

She had sent for me
To examine it. Let it be
for visitors, she said.

She passed a message to the nursery:
The child must look less intense
When she listens to music.

I bought my mother a china boot
covered with flowers.
It was not her favourite ornament

Illustration by Eric J. Proctor
Photographed by Simon Heron

FRIENDS

Sent out to play for two hours each morning
in my tight-fitting, velvet-collared coat,
I would stand under the catalpa tree
and think.

When Pullen the gardener came down
from the loggia with a full watering can,
I asked him why he leaned to one side.
He answered me and smiled.

Matthewman, a giant in dungarees, who
attended to the boiler and did odd jobs,
would stand astride the back path
with a quiet hum or whistle.

I thought of the 'ragamuffin'
I met in the Broad Walk.
How could we play - with my
coat so hard to unbutton?

FITTING IN

This square peg
Had a refined origin,
good education
And suitable marriage -

Pre-natal exercises
After prolonged and painful labour,
eased the birth of a son

Who developed schizophrenia
And shared with his mother
Gifts of understanding
As well as harsh conflict.

The peg has now been
smoothly shaved
At the four corners of moral
and intellectual yearning,
erring belief
And inappropriate affection.

There is hope that
Once planted in the round hole,
A grace of words will grow.

FALL

My heart is glad for unfolding reasons -
Through shocks to a faith which sickness betrayed.
Autumn shakes free the fruit from its own season.

Son, brother, mother knew the mind's recession.
Father, wine-filled, loved the child he portrayed.
My heart is glad for unfolding reasons.

Though dressed in silk for party occasions
Alone I heard a horn concerto played.
Autumn shakes free the fruit from its own season.

A married sister shone through warm expressions
And to me, a girl, fitful love conveyed.
My heart is glad for unfolding reasons.

Untouched by parental taste, my selection
Might be of Machaut, Herbert and Paul Klee.
Autumn shakes free the fruit from its own season.

Thought can transcend moods of deep dejection
While natural death can scarcely be delayed.
My heart is glad for unfolding reasons.
Autumn shakes free the fruit from its own season.

*Painting of author as a child in a Dutch costume in
1937 by her father, Eric J.Proctor*

Photographed by Simon Heron

FOR ANNE

St. Francis of Assisi,
unlike other saints
Cherished what he called

"Brother body"
Although I'm old
And glad of my thoughts

I have not wished my mind
wrested from my body
For the sake of argument.

Old people still love
and have the right to.
In me sexual desire

Developed late. I expect
no response beyond the cold
label "inappropriate".

My youth was spent,
contrary to custom,
repeatedly playing LPs

of Mozart,
Bach
and Buxtehude.

HELLO AND GOODBYE AT THE AIRPORT

Shall I put my unwanted love
In the pocket of my loose cream jeans
(Bought to make a carefree impression)
And leave them hanging?

First to arrive on the airport bus,
I felt an old friend's ambiguous hug.
Then, at the end of the course,
Approaching the barrier where we waited to board

And before a line-up of women,
I turned energetically
This way and that
Trying to escape the final embrace

Which, when it came
I wanted to make
More than it was.

IN HAYCOMBE CEMETERY, BATH
TO A PSYCHOANALYST

The cold wind bit
and blew awry my bunch of roses
as we walked
towards the grave.

I laid them sideways
And saw they did not count,
although I had enjoyed
their beauty on the way.

The granite tombstone moved me
with its plain statement
of the nature of his work,

And then the names
of children -
Three of them unknown.

At last, the line from Dylan Thomas
seemed to show him angry
when approaching death,

but did not change
the prevailing sense of goodness
I had always felt.

INCLEMENT WEATHER

Gales have inclined a tree
from growing upright
to a glorious arc.

My tree of life
has lost some branches
and felt the drought.

The tree was bent
by 'a narrow wind'
and the sky's comment.

I have learned
to praise
Afforestation

to catch a blue satin cloth
enclosed in a parcel
with a mention of rain.

LATE DEVELOPMENT IN MARRIAGE

His persistence captured her in old age.
After years of gifts of flowers, heavy
housework and polishing of glass,
he continued wooing by cassettes of Don Giovanni,
Hindu and Armenian chants -

it had been to her a kind of foreplay.
When young, in fear and ignorance,
she'd turned away,
except when clamouring for a child.

Now she enjoys his fine-veined thigh, white feet,
chest woven with a bird's first house mesh.
She's glad to please a husband
who in love is sensitive to time,
and once ordained good silences for reading.

MOTHER'S DAY

Thirty years to learn to hold an infant,
not my own now but Luke, son of a friend,
Peter slipped in sucking and had known want.

Photographs show a head with sparse hair bent
over the friend's young child with tenderness.
My cold touch with Peter I failed to mend -

Later gave my son his favourite dishes,
shy kisses, then a bowl of primulas;
frequently listened with uneasiness.

Did my holding him seem precarious,
my love remote like some fragile cumulus?

OLD AGE IN CLONBARRA

Sun, flecked with rain, sweeps across the garden,
Touches a bird tray with plant in hanging bowl.
Rage at my declining asks for a midden.
There's none to take the grossness of my soul.
Limpid water from the old boot on the path
Won't wash me nor what's filtered absolve me -
Coming from the jug that stands near the hearth.
Madly the hen bucket yawns to receive me.
A diary for 2002 changed my mood.
I had to smile or invisibly weep.
Errors about others' ages were withstood
with unmannerly firmness and love running deep.
On being told a joke about a rope
And a cow, I was filled with newborn hope.

SINGLE TRACK - A POET'S

The track of the writer
is furrowed and potholed -

One day she will cherish her family
by watering the humidifiers
or listening quietly -
by preparing mauve and white turnips
or poaching eggs in the simple way.

On the next she'll vanish
To write at her desk.

My own track lies in not emulating
better cooks and cleaners
nor thorough paper readers.

Not shunning people for solitude.
Nor solitude for people -

Wanting always
to be alone with my mind.

THE WATER GARDEN

It was not a well-cultivated plot of land, rather a wilderness. The grass was lush and always wet; blue and yellow iris shone out against dark undergrowth; flowers of the American Currant lit up like pink stars. From the little gate the ground sloped downward. At the foot of a stream lords and ladies with yellow-green trumpets stood erect. Water cress thrived in the clear water by the well, now closed in. The well seemed slightly sinister and I wondered whether it led to the secret passage supposed to run from somewhere in the grounds to the house. Next was the small swimming pool, converted from an aquarium. The water was cold because of an overhanging tree. I used to enjoy Spartan bathes in the morning before school. Near the fence at the bottom was the winding tributary of the Medway. The waters ran slowly and I imagined they were those by which the Lord would lead me, as in the 23rd Psalm. Meanwhile I devoted myself to digging up clay from the bed of the streams to make thumb and coil pots. I wept when they cracked in the oven.

To the left was a large pond, retreat of moorhens. I would look for their nests, jump across to a little island and go tadpoling. Sometimes I noticed the white belly of a dead frog or heard the slither of a grass snake. Water lilies lay on the pond but it was still wild not formal.

Nearby, in the marshiest part of the garden, grew rhubarb leaves which we called elephant leaves. My sister put one in our parents' bed as a joke.

These were joys but the water garden also witnessed pain. Once the bar of an improvised swing hurt my mouth. Then when the cuckoo called incessantly and cuckoo flowers were sprinkled everywhere, I tried to strangle myself being disappointed by a school friend. I wrote my last message in green crayon on cartridge paper. I intimated that I expected to go to heaven but if my brother had not kindly interrupted me, I might have haunted the ground which has since haunted me.

THREE POPPIES

Suddenly they flared out
With petals of pale orange.
I watched their life,
Perfect on the first day,
On the second their edges
Tinged with grey.

The wind blew,
The third day.
Those petals fell
And started to decay -
Their beauty
A transient display.

BALLYCONNELL

After we had driven
through overarching beeches
down a winding road,
we came to an almost hidden path.

My host's son, my guide,
bounded along it like a deer,
to see where it went.
Satisfied, he led me to the grave.

By the path, deep in the woods,
yellow celandine were growing,
bluebells and rhododendrons.
We came to a circular

black-railinged garden -
mostly overgrown -
with a little gate.
In the middle was a headstone

on which was written,
'Sir John Olphert
died, March 1917.'
It said that he wished

to be buried in his garden
among his flowers.
Legend allows him
a hound on either side.

Standing on a large rock in Ballyconnell
he knew he was lord as far as eye could see.
Yet he paid his work people
with small bags of flour.

When the labourers rose up
indignantly, he allotted a strip
of land to each family
and with a little English fairness

measured Irish acreage
according to the number
of heads in each group.
Still, he'd worked his people hard.

Did his good and kindly wife
compose his epitaph
or did he devise it himself
in hope of being loved at last?

AFTER 'DECORUM'

I am in love with a surrounding
of walnut or teak furniture,
thick woollen rugs,
a silver dish or pewter bowl,
lively papered or coloured walls
with paintings or artistic prints.

I like flexible manners,
ill-feeling contained,
criticism considered,
grief acknowledged,
speech modulated,
jokes that work without hurt.

I want to know how to use
the myriad words I've read,
the words I've heard and overheard,
proper words and swearwords,
slang, native idiom and foreign imports,
words I've traced in reference books.

A QUIET FESTIVAL

I went to Salzburg from a house in Notting Hill
because I liked music and to be alone.
To spare myself and them
I did not tell my parents
I would be on my own.

The outskirts hotel was whitewashed.
Lonely in the dining room
I showed crumpled tickets in my hand
And asked the way to Mozart; then chanced upon
the unfolding of Mahler's Song of the Earth.

In the afternoons I did a watercolour
of a prancing horse -a sculpture on the fountain -
in tender shades of blue and ochre;
or wandered to the silent boathouse
beside the Wolfgangsee.

I returned to my home in Notting Hill
happy with a week's changes of thought,
glad now of daily conversation.
Yet here was no music but what I played
in my room on wireless and gramophone.

ALIENATION

Keen gusts assail me;
with no bus stop to identify me,
I put one arm round a lampost,
the other holds my French beret to my head.
My hair blows out in strands,
feet are numb and hands losing their grip.
I watch complacent drivers
with half empty cars
pass by and ignore me.
Wind does not abate.
Hailstones sting me.

ANCIENT ROME, 1996

The vigour of the Colosseum
Real, despite late moral judgment,
And the beauty of the Roman Forum -
Ruins interspersed with fresh green slopes,
Each with a pine for focus -
Contrast with the neglectful air
Around the Imperial Forum
With its duller-coloured brick
And senseless scattering
Of broken architraves;
Graffiti-smothered notices
And indifferent pedestrians.
Only Trajan's column
Still seems noble.

STRANDHILL, SLIGO

The old student was left in the car
by her own prompting and agreement
while the middle-aged strode off
into the sunset and along the beach.

Mussorgski's "Pictures at an Exhibition",
played by a brass band, came across on
Lyric FM. Even this version brought
familiar pleasure, and Pergolesi,
sung by soprano, Emma Kirkby, supreme
delight. Shostakovich which followed
signalled doubt. She switched off the radio
and looked through the windscreen.

Moved by manifold changes of the sky
and wanting cold air, she got out
and stood in the wind.

FAREWELL IRELAND

Ireland of wild flowers: daisies,
    dandelions and violets
    - hardy gorse.

Ireland of greetings from car driver,
publican or woman in the street.

Ireland of changing skies, yellow grey,
blue grey, mackerel, white, azure -
and the promised emerald fields.

Farewell to Muckish and Errigal, fearsome mountains,
and to weather-torn prospects through the window.
Farewell to fuchsia in the hedgerows,
warm in colour - is it wild?

Farewell St. Patrick's Day and my first hot whiskey.
Farewell to children on the float,
peeping from beneath their shamrock hats,
waiting to dance in the rain.

Farewell to quarter bottles of wine
and walking arm-in-arm
with an Irish singer on each side.
Farewell to Irish courtesy
and respect for modesty.

Farewell to mute swans on the lake.
Farewell to small houses with painted facades
and gravel yards, raked and garnished.
Farewell to market towns.

Farewell to stubborn sheep and black-legged lambs.
Farewell to boulders
and the dun hillside.

Farewell to meeting an Irish stranger
wanting to know the way of me as I of him.
Farewell our talk of Seamus Heaney.

Farewell to fluent speech
and the witty rejoinder.
Farewell Ireland.

CANADA GOOSE

I am as big as a three-year-old child
That knows its power to manipulate.
I sing a noisy song of search
That ends in private gardens.
I am not a coo-er, a bleeper or a whistler.
I move from the north and try to assimilate.

I smell with a no-fragrance smell
And feed on submerged fish and larvae.
At night I hide on the island
And cover my head with my wings.
I dream of the far away north
and deeper and fuller water.

I worship the safety of the gaggle
Its number and freedom from hurt.

Deep mauve, silver and red
We fly in a crowd
Ceaselessy turning.

CARPE DIEM

Gorse in flower
has its interior light.
Past and future teach me
that the thorns are sharp.

ENCOUNTER IN THE ROUND ROOM, DARTINGTON

A girl with short dark hair
laid aside her backpack
and paused for tea.
After she had stowed her map
we spoke of a poem
that filled the day.

Then she withdrew into herself
her head held high,
a Viking prow,
fixed her pack
and walked away.

CLOAK OF MOTHERHOOD

It rained on Peter's thirtieth birthday,
Rained all morning - and he thought
The *Peter Rabbit* greeting card
The church sent him, mocked his childish traits.
Some blood-red halves of grapefruit
Reminded him of the child
His girlfriend aborted.

* * *

Though his mother regretted
His greasy hair growing at odds
Like a dead tulip turned inside out,
His ragged shirt flaunting
A supposed neglect.
Manner brusque and ungracious.
Goodness veiled. Suppressed.

This was her teenage son
With whom her love
Will never be done.

* * *

He gave her two kisses
Perfect and natural in turn.
In uneasy greed she demanded a third.
It was like spilling ink
On a delicate sketch.

Winged in a cycle crash
He returns captive to the nest
With the precious gift
Of four days' recovered motherhood.
He asks her to sit with him,
To read his favourite story
Of Samson and Delilah
From the children's Bible.
He recalls boyhood friends
And incidents
While demanding comforts and food.
They dabble in pools of forgotten love.
She is warmed.
She is stretched. She unbends.
She rejoices.
Adolescent shouts are stilled.

CLOAK II

Is the wind on the common
Making her weep?

He wants to leave home
Because of his uncongenial parents,
Because of the pressure they exert.
Because of their aura
He can't work.
He can only smoke
And listen to his Music Centre.

If she asks a question
She interferes,
So that's the end of communication.

No it's not the wind on the common
Making her weep.

* * *

She wants to die in the marriage bed,
Facing the 'View of Delft'
With the Samuel Palmer-like
Pastel above her head;
On another wall a young painter's
Wild gouache of Spain;
The long window by her side
Giving her sky, a tall fir
And bare branches of young oaks.

She'd like to be able
Still to ponder
How they held hands all night
Wondering if their son still lived.

* * *

The garden bench is placed across
The corner, between the cypress hedge
And the bed of delphiniums -
Sturdy with a back of wrought iron,
A seat of light wood struts.

CLOAK III

He had seen it on the pavement
Outside a shop that promised savings,
Called his parents to view it,
Prevailed on his father to buy.
His mother blessed him as usual,
While his father declined to be seated.

At home at weekends
The young man would withdraw
to the bench to smoke -
Either to strengthen a quarrel
Or to worship the sun

For his mother on weekdays
The bench took on a charm
Equal to all his father's husbandry.

* * *

Her love for her son
Has exceeded all parallel loves
His love for her,
Once shown with brown suede gloves
Lined with creamy fleece,
Has deepened -
To allow her freedom
To lose them without notice,
And to wear red wool ones

She could not navigate
The sea of evil-sounding words
That surged before he said
"I love you more than anybody" -
Which brought her to port.

* * *

The white china clock
covered with roses,
A gift of filial love,
Stopped at six-thirty -

CLOAK IV

Then started again,
Continuing
Slowly - uncertain, fitful

God forbid it should cease
She thought.

* * *

On her desk-stand between a glass penguin
And black ball-point pen, her son's kiosk photo
Confers a joy by lips still rose, frank eyes
Untidy hair in chestnut tufts, warm skin.
Now his jagged soul resides within
A stronger frame of monumental limbs.
Regimes of beer and smoking, bread and cheese,
Self-given burns on hand and marks on neck,
Clumsy jabs by which healing drugs can be applied,
Have not, she finds, constrained his wit and kindness.

* * *

She'd throw away the cloak of motherhood,
Worn out with care and sorrow
And don a more exotic robe
Woven of the flame
Of pride and self-determination,
Fringed with creative urges to write and paint.
She'd be whole and not fragmented.
An integrated person

But what's the use?
The threadbare cloak
Has stuck to her flesh,
And she must wear it
To the end.

WHAT HE LEFT BEHIND

Twelve black sacks
from his sheltered flat,
clustered like ravens -

four days to empty and sort
weeks to sift and distribute,
the rest of life to ponder.

Greeting cards, some hand-done,
from cousins, friends
and workmates;

a new task for parents
tired out with sorrow
and long anxious days.

A few non-perishable foodstuffs, sugar,
crisps and Golden Shred we started
to eat as though he'd returned to feed us.

The grief of doctor, community psychiatric
nurse, was also felt by the outreach worker,
frustrated in his rainbow-like ideas.

On The Way From The Crematorium Vault

A young man, soberly dressed, his moustache red roses, came up from oblivion, carrying ashes in a deep cardboard box. The signing of a receipt disturbed the angels who hate formality.

He led the old couple to the Hall of Memory where a lady in a pale turquoise coat fluttered away from the Book of Remembrance in its glass cabinet and left. The young man pointed to the book and made long claims about the medieval flourishes and emblems that could be added to mourning inscriptions.

The old couple walked down the narrow road between turf and stone, sometimes startled by a car engine. The man carried the heavy cardbox with their son's ashes inside a shabby emerald bag. The woman took the weight at the round-about but fear of injuring herself made her give it back.

Suddenly Camilla, a tiny infant, appeared on the grass, then vanished behind her tombstone. The old woman saddened while her man watched. Were short joys, short griefs better?

Further on were pansies, small crosses, piles of earth, a life that continued in burying the dead. Outside the gate, the bus stop.

FANTASY IN THE ALGARVE

Will you emerge from behind a palm
at this unlikely tropical venue -
disshevelled, full-girthed, deep-chested -
engage with the children of Silves,
charm them with gifts and humour
and be a child with them -
then disappear -while they remain,
a blessing to their mothers?

RELAY RACE

Memory holds the spirit -
memory falters,
then deteriorates.

It is said 'The exit is farewell
but every exit is an entry -
an entry for the living'.

Each player passes on his message
and the touch and exchange
either warm the heart
or chill it like summer sleet.

LULLABY

Peeling apples, week in, week out,
Adding ginger, also sugar, then some water,
Stewing gently for a while,
And so to bed and sleep.

Straightening sheets, day in, day out,
Fluffing pillows, smoothing blankets, ironing clothes,
Talking quietly for a while
And so to bed and sleep.

Drawing curtains, year in, year out,
Oiling locks and hinges,
Tying dead heads in the garden,
Dusting frames in black and gold,
Then musing for a while
And so to bed and sleep.

CHANCE AND CHANGE - TEASPOONS

A silver spoon, a birth gift;
The plated meant for humbling;
Six stylish stainless steel,
Armenian - full, ornate.

They press herbal with honey,
Cocoa with milk and sugar,
Brazilian grains with ice,
Lemonade with rind and pulp.

Old age is comprehended
And the childish palate pleased
Initiative survives
While bitterness adds to taste.

BIRTH ANNOUNCEMENT

Glad that she survived
births and miscarriages,
that he is big and well.

Hard to have heard
just by a card
not by a call.

Sibling's eighth grandchild -
for our sole foetus
the death bell tolled.

Who bears the child?
Who writes the picture?
Who paints the poem?

APPROACHING DEATH

Two movements conflict in old age:
The regressive: seeking youth again
By an overactive life style
And a demand for total recall;
while the natural or divine
Encroaches on the body:
On the eyes, the ears, the limbs,
Texture and pigmentation of skin;
And on the mind:
Causing faulty memory
And incoherence.

Both movements affect
Security of Tenure -
One tries to maintain it,
The other to weaken.

I hope
To loosen my foothold
And wait.

FALLING

A steel wire ball
becomes unravelled
as it rubs against false argument
by some who preach or advertise.

Not seeking a perfect experience
it picks up recorded Monteverdi
and can't pass by a Whistler print
on account of his mistress' tranquil pose.

Its threads part in a smile
on hearing Guillaume de Machaut
sound strains of earthly love
with virgin adulation.

The steel wire ball
tumbles down with shocks and pauses
hard with ambition
round with a sense of the good.

WISHFUL THINKING

I heard quick footsteps
coming to the door
and knew they were not his,
yet hoped until
the swish of the letterbox
showed it was the postman,
that love and long experience
could err.

NO PROBLEM

I shall not switch the light off or on.
I shall not stub my toes on a projection
nor enter an argument
too balanced for conclusion.

I shall not gobble my food
nor drink tea or coffee out of turn.
Others may smile or frown.
They will work the urn.

PARK GATE, SOUTH-WESTERN HEALTH TRUST

The new sign leads to the Limbless Centre,
then across a space for staff cars only
to the back entrance
of the Psychiatric Ward.

Here is no green sward,
or pond with ducks. No gravel
paths with beds of growing
flowers or noble trees.

Contrary to what the public expects
punch-ups are rare
so are screams and
irrational speech.

Here there is lounging and weeping,
pacing and sauntering.
A nurse will also patrol the ward.
Others huddle behind Reception.

THE MINDER

I can still see a photograph
of my curly-headed son
with two or three other kids
whose presences are blank.
Peter looked bonny and pleased
in front of a council house -
petunias leaning over from a window box.

I wasn't allowed to mother my son
because I fell ill with recurring
depression after his birth.

Once on return from France,
we guessed that Joyce,
his minder, a wife, neat and comely,
had borrowed our master bedroom
for a night with her lover.

On final parting
Joyce gave me a slice of lemon
for the backs of my hands:
'To whiten them', she said.

Death at Naz-dessus

I would go with you,
Duncan's mother,
as a mother also,
like Ruth with Naomi,
to hear the River Allondon, see the field,
its scattered yellow rocks.

In that blocked off
wilderness of France
to which there is no road,
one walker found him,
fallen between two stones.
Two others passed nearby.

The body of your son
Would seem to me like Peter's
Your grief my grief -
I share your doubt
as to why Duncan died.
Peter followed soon with a certain leap.

AFTER MY SON'S DEMISE

Lilies belied his death's malice:
consolation was sprinkled from clouds.
I received a surfeit of mothering
in hugs and unexpected kisses,
chocolates, phone calls and 'wise' sayings.

Photos of unexpected mourners
appeared among shots of cherished bouquets.
Then a deluge of silence.

THE BALANCE OF HIS MIND

Despite his loving gifts
he said at last:

Why did you go on drinking tea
when I came home from school?
Why were you so uncaring?
How can you drink it now?
You have ruined my life.

A Bereaved Mother Contemplates the Ancient Hymn 'O Sacred Head'

The wounds from a bleeding head look obscene
Not holy: Each mother is a Mary
To her vulnerable child. Impious, contrary,
She turns away from the thorn-piercing scene

And ponders what her son's joyful birth could mean -
'Comeliness and vigour' proved a vagary,
But the drift of the hymn is luminary
Addressing death as though he might be seen.

'Death's pallid hue' she felt she had witnessed
And was shamed by her son's bloated figure,
Saddened by the mocking of faith he'd caught.

The later words of the hymn brought her rest.
Despite her cast of mind's sceptic rigour
The archetypal shepherd was whom she sought.

FOR MAURA

The wind howls,
the stove is cold,
pampas grass shakes.
The meaning of life
seems centred in the pink hyacinth
on the windowsill
because of its feel and growth.

While you find solace in a wake,
your tragedy leaves me alone
thinking of an earlier sorrow,
more stark because the kinship was closer
and the death, self-inflicted,
left peculiar hurts.

I hear your niece shone with beauty, intelligence,
good humour, high spirits and health.
These qualities in Peter were slowly eroded.
All we could share was grief.

Lament

I crouch in the corner with dust and dirt.
There is grass for the others
with trees and ornamental benches.

When the rest wander away
I lie under a tree and uncurl
my fingers like fronds.

If I stand up and stretch,
a voice calls his sheer
jump from the fire escape
a warning of his last desperate act.
I thought the branch and leaf
survive together.

ON THE DISTRICT LINE

Parsons Green
Behind the blatant sign
are railings painted Royal Blue -
of a cruder shade
than I've seen before -
behind the railings, evergreens -
I wish to God they also died.

Parsons Green
A witness saw him run
beside the yellow line, before his jump,
flapping his arms as though to fly.

Parsons Green
We feared the transit but habit prevailed -
concerts, lectures, West End stores.
When the train stops, we bow our heads,
study the printed page.

THE VISIT

By the lack of a remorseful 'phone call from my son after the abuse he uttered, I was warned of the coming of police. Early in the morning the door bell rang. My husband descended slowly after me.

I could not envisage the scene in our home. I thought I was at the police station in a bare triangular room with deep windows to let in the sun. My husband went up to the two police, man and woman. They said Peter was dead. I moved about, sat on a bench, a chair or stool, suspecting faintness. Unheeded, I joined the group who stood in the centre in a kind of arabesque.

The police gave us details of how Peter went from the hospital to Parsons Green station and died of head injuries as he jumped before the engine of a moving train. They advised us not to see the body - we never did. From the police's quiet demeanour I learned to respect the dead.

BETWEEN BEECH AND OAK

No more symbols, links or aide-memoires,
no pains in the womb or itches on the chest
where cancer took the right-hand breast.

In youth milk failed from a body said
to give a babe an awkward hold.

Hands that cradled timidly
are now adroit with word machine
and kitchen knife.

Eyes that looked for childhood patterns,
observe the moods in strangers' faces,

watch the trees that grow upright.
As rain dampens earth and leaves,
the ashes do not quicken.

FRENCH CAFÉ IN CLAPHAM

Sitting in Café Délice
looking through the window and up the road,
I thought I saw,
behind the dense cover of clouds,
a pale blue sky.
This was my imagining, this my hope
after the death of my son.

On the pavement a thin coat of stubs and litter,
smart young women standing
with expressionless faces;
others confident, hurrying to work,
children with top knots,
linked to their mothers
or darting ahead.

Suddenly clouds, parting like ballerinas,
left Wilde's 'little tent of blue' to fill the sky.
People spoke of the change with delight.
Most weathers might be more temperate
than mine - yet everybody suffers,
grows fearful, tired disconsolate
and wants a blue canopy or heaven.

I Am Comforted

Three years after Peter's suicide
I dreamed I laid white crocuses
in damp earth beyond the styx.
When I reached that far bank
I found them plucked and lying on the grass.

I left them there
and returned from hell,
planted tiny bulbs for purple flowers.

Balm and Stings

How can we inherit from our son
his gift for finding words in the face of death:
the fitting phrase when a mate was lost;
the way he wrote condolences to my delicate friend
when her army husband died of a cancer
he was sure he would conquer; the way he
tenderly circled the waist of his aunt
after a gruff grandfather expired at last.

Can Peter's forbearance of the old man's ill-temper
heal our minds with his spirit
when he has destroyed his young body
and left us lying on a bed of nettles?

THREE ANGLES OF PERCEPTION

The murky bog is studded with pools.
I love the silence of the sheep, turned one way,
the no-lorry, no-tractor silence.
Yet when I look towards the mountains,
The whole is fearful and without solution.

I listen to the noise of Rachmaninov,
perfection of a Bach partita,
The confident, full-blooded compere
also promoting hand-made chocolates.
The whole's in fragments and without solution.

The bus passes boulders, shining lake and river.
I notice the pure faces of schoolgirls
and marvel how to each as she alights
the driver addresses an appropriate farewell -
a numinous solution.

To God in Modern Times

Lord, how shall I pray? Shall I weary you
With grocery list of body and soul,
Repeat fear and need as the faithless do
Or hide my grief in sacramental bowl?
Shall I forget singing of summer lark,
How the stars lighten, the touch of man's hand,
Smell of new bread? Wrapped in cathedral dark,
My taper of love is smothered not fanned.
The dried flowers of liturgical chants
Give out no scent. I think that you perceive
And love without our words. I will dance
To the humming world, finding space to grieve.
Lord, rhythm of earth is enough for me;
I'll listen and measure and taste and see.

BEATING DOWN THE BRAMBLES

The Muslim faith gives glory to the godhead
Keeps woman in subjection,
Stresses prayer by repetition
And physical prostration;
Honours beauty.

Christ gave us thoughts of love
Of the enemy but negated them
With the promise of coals of fire on his head.
He ordered shaking off the dust at sceptics' doors,
And self-denial - which can lead to self-neglect.

The Buddha was noble, ascetic and giving,
Commending a sense of everything dying
To prepare us for a death
Relieved by
Hope of rebirth.

Hindu chanting glorifies Siva
The inner self or consciousness.
Thus God in essence
Brings joy and peace -
So evil melts away.

Since the apple does not fall far from the tree
The Judaic-Christian scriptures
Will always be close,
Not forgetting the prophet Freud,
But I stake a claim to be eclectic,
To work out my own life pattern.

The Underground

Is it sad
that I climb the broken escalator?
that I watch with pleasure
a hobo on the train
beside a self-rocking pram?

Is it sad
that seeing young men and children
sitting down,
I feel shot with pain
in neck and thighs
till, as I struggle with my glasses case,
an observant man
gives up his seat with grace?

METAMORPHOSIS INTO HERRING

Press your useless arms to your side,
Squeeze your legs together.
Sink your head into your body.
Keep your eyes wide open
for later on, when death comes
through the net.

Receive the silver spray,
the coating of your flesh -
above the world the sound of singing -
a soft roe perhaps for female young.
Below the water the bliss of swimming
while you approach but slip by other fish.

TROLLS

Trolls shake their feet in the stream.
They splash you and slash your boots.
They cannot be half-witted
as the people loosely maintain:
evil comes from a clever brain.

In Scandinavia they had figured
as giants of heathen myth,
of sceptical imagination.
They lost status by failing
to unseat Thor - as mascots were blamed for souls ailing.

The confraternity of evil spirits
who sometimes put on bodies
include Puck, gremlins, people of the Kalevala,
Satan of sculptural magnificence,
enemies coming from our mind's incontinence.

Trolls are small, though sometimes three-headed,
their torsoes twist around the trellis
and shrivel the winter jasmine.
Warming milk is turned off as covertly they creep
and shift your pillow when you try to sleep.

VASES MOSTLY UNDER THE SINK

A tiny brown thumbpot with a hole for a flower
such as pansy or winter jasmine,
Lalique glass with bas-relief of Caryatides
pouring water - graceful with roses -
a pottery cylinder
for a handful of freesia,
small china vase
painted with an indefinite dahlia
for wild flowers
like germander speedwell or creeping thistle.

A big fresh version of a bowl
with deep brown and turquoise below the glaze,
being modern, needs no flower.

EVALUATION AND MOURNING

I judge myself daily -
so do friends and relations -
no need to wait till crack of doom.

From my dead loved ones
I've heard no sound,
only a breath of opinion

that I should read
raptures of Swinburne, follow
rhythms of Villa-Lobos,

finger linen, try 2B pencils
for household lists,
gulp a glass of Burgundy
and maintain integrity.

MY SISTER AS CHRISTMAS TREE ANGEL

She brought a taste of joy on entering
a home where we were sometimes sombre,
mother or son experiencing mental anguish,
father holding his own with reserve.
No Christmas decorations, not a pudding to be stirred.

In loose-fitting renaissance velvet
my sister moved between the rise and fall
of each level of language.
My son's was intelligent but streetwise,
his father's quiet and urbane,
my speech staccato,
without the grace to cover
moments of malaise.

My sister praised my son's tree
on a greeting card
propped against presents.
She'd brought for him a roomy jacket,
for his father short black umbrella and gloves,
for me an antique tear bottle,
a jar of homemade jam
and a bunch of peach carnations.
By her wisdom and bounty my sister
made the locked gates open.

To a Dear Investment Analyst

You show your love
in everyday exchanges
by prompt repayment
of each debt.

Scrutinizing
financial papers
frustrates small talk,
needs concentration,

which you apply as well
to making soup or appraising
fringe theatre, tragic opera
or Far Eastern film.

When I looked in the magnifying glass
and observed the 'ravages of time'
you bought me a bunch of iris,
my favourite flower.

I cannot fault your meditation;
for every hour it takes,
you cheerfully fulfil
a thousand thankless tasks.

You love your car
and warm it underneath
with four
well tended burners.

You like to stride
across the Common,
still mourning the dog
who once walked beside you.

HOMAGE TO KLORANDA

You brought us little known flowers
with strong stems, orange and pink petals.
Your head and smooth dark hair
were beautiful, limbs like those of Greek statues.
You knew and imparted calmness and repose.

You iron like other women
but the making of your daughter's dresses
shows professional art.
Quick to observe
the needs of your children,

Klaus, Klaudja and Flavio
with here a kiss, a touch,
a hug - or even angry word -
you also feed them by thoughtful measure,
not forgetting to spread
your husband's slice with cheese.

INTEGRITY

Five-year-old Kosovan Klaus
crayoned a picture of our house
showing a bunch of flowers above it.

Klaus's parents had brought separate
bouquets; for their host carnations and fern;
for me Gypsophila and yellow roses.

His parents asked,
'Would you like to stay here?'
Klaus shyly shook his head

Later my husband sellotaped the drawing
to the wall. He had given me
fresh tulips to replace dead buds.

ELEGY FOR MADGE, A JEWISH AUNT

The tall house is empty now
Like your tall body. Your will
No longer hurries thin ankles
To the door to welcome us.

All the contents are dispersed.
A colour-washed plaster bust
Shows your time of gentle youth -
With age you grew in subtle spice.

From the brown album sisters
gaze, calm but coyly vieing.
They had their families
You your secret fears and sprees.

The tall house had many rooms
But you lived in a small one -
The black room at the back
Where bulbs could never flower.

Yet there was a happy flight;
At the top, not out of reach.
A wry china elephant
Lorded the ascent.

Though your worldly goods are gone,
Fragments of your soul remain.
You bequeathed to us a room
Built on grief to play the fool.

SUZANNA

I like this baby with wide apart eyes,
not a stranger but related.

She sits on my lap in long quiet,
then moves about good-naturedly.
I think she's lent as my retreat.

ELEGY FOR AN ART DEALER

Gustav Delbanco
Arrived from Hamburg
In the 1930s,

One of three founders of a London
Gallery in Cork Street,
Told a young doctor

At the end,
That he was 'G. Delbanco -
A nonentity'.

He would not have relished hearing
That his goodness deserved
His ninety-three years.

He could be rude or outspoken,
Interrupting conversations
Or remarking too frankly on dress.

I recall a range of learning -
Expressed with solecisms -
About Durer, Burne-Jones and Picasso;

And the young
Whom he loved
Whether gifted or not,

And what I prized the most
While I struggled with typing
Were kind but witty insights

Which led him once to fetch,
As solace for my weeping,
'A masterpiece of a pear'.

UNRULY GARDEN

Not wanting to forgo his touch
I'm afraid, though he's now asleep,
to leave him for the garden -
with its burgundy dahlias,
rain daisies and orange-scarlet chaenomeles.

I do not overpraise his garden
nor would I have him admire to excess
my fish dishes nor tea ritual.
I would rather we ceased
to adore each other's gifts.

Believing what was not spoken of
in my childhood home, must be evil,
I always feared sexual love.
Impotence in marriage was mutual and
hormone treatment curtails a man's desire.

I grew old.
His love of kitchen work increased
like his love of the tango.
I feel the grace and action of the dance
possessed him. He used to say,

"Young girls are like blossoms".
It felt like a drenching shower.
He would also brush past me unaware.
Yet we had given birth to a son,
chestnut-haired, lively in humour

and conversation. He later took his life.
We none of us rest in Nature.
Perhaps our grief and sense of failure
stopped more flowering.
I only know my body feels the cold.

SEMBLANCE OF A DAUGHTER-IN-LAW

She was pale and thin
hands and arms self-scored with cuts,
body clothed in black,
long silky skirt,
deep rose anorak.

I liked her dusky hair
and unmixed feelings:
fondness for our son, her lover,
hatred for her husband's mistress,
yet loyalty to rejecting spouse,

warmth to her new-found parents
to whom she gave a picture of puppies
and a graceful spray
of artificial flowers -

for our aborted grandchild
Was a shared unspoken grief.

THOUGHTS WHILE AWAY

Milk in a toothmug
A tea strainer on the bedroom stool
Curtains rich and dark like tapestry
Yet without images
The young but weathered Persian rug
With blue spot against the Evil Eye
Deep stained parquet floor
And stricken amaryllis
With leaves askew and no flower

I do not miss my home
And yet it crowds my mind.

LETTER TO MY SON WHO DIED IN *1999*, AGED *32*

My dear Peter,

I built a memorial garden for you
with five plants in the brown waste
between dahlias, still in leaf,
and the cypress hedge.
A tobacco plant grows tall and smells sweet -
for those who can smell it -
a reminder of your life habit.

Lobelias on each side
make me think of Joan's eyes
though I don't recall their colour.
The French lavender represents
the frailty of your ego
together with a toughness
in the upshooting petal.
Bright pink Busy Lizzie illustrates
your love of genial pubs
and all things British.

I water it most days.

THE SUNKEN GARDEN

Night dreams are the flowers
Whose blooms give light to leaden day
Along the paths and against the ledges
Of damp, uneven stone.

Sometimes I stand
By the central urn
Where tulips thrust upward,
And watch how the paths converge
Between beds of wallflowers
Fragrant and still,
Double-hued fuchsia, pink and puce,
Forget-me-nots in profusion;
All trying to grow
Above the garden walls.

And sometimes
I stand under the willow
Seeking the shelter of prayer.

But there are benches
By the edge of the sunken garden,
And often I sit and wonder
Who are the gardeners
And when will it rain?

WOUNDS AND POWER

I was alone
In a well-tended garden
Two hours at a time,
Angry and hurt.

I was alone
In a maze of streams
Beside the Medway,
Dreaming and making pots.

I was alone
In my house
With bookshelves and music
Quiet and happy.

I was alone
With people who listened,
My thoughts now accepted
Now rebounding.

VICISSITUDES

You took yourself off
to tend the sweet peas.
I wanted to show you my black doll
whom I could undress from her handknitted clothes.
you were my mother.

You took me off
to pubs to discuss your nervous amours.
Though your penchant was science
You gave me poetry books.
You were my brother.

You took me off
to Espresso bars, unashamed of clothed caresses;
We became engaged; my parents declined
to receive us for dinner.
You were my lover.

You fobbed me off
with fortnightly lunches,
Live in your digs, your University
lectures. You talked of new girl-friends.
I was almost a sister.

I took myself off,
struck out on my own.
You married first,
We both married wisely.
We were our own true lovers.

DALLIANCE

There were snowdrops,
Tall trees, grassy slopes.
It was cold but sunny.
The pond was marked
With a notice saying 'Poison'.

I saw small children playing,
Old couples walking.
The verges were neatly cut.
Firm-petalled camellias grew there
and an early rhododendron.

A man, with his wife trailing,
Noticed my pleasure and spoke of them.
I had felt alone and chilly -
Without my husband.

07.07.05

I saw the blackened faces in the underground though I was only travelling after the explosion of the bombs. Next day it was remarkable how most young people, men and girls alike, wore black - upright in their posture, fearful in their eyes.

On the day itself a rendezvous had been arranged between my lacanian analyst and myself with the object of exploring Kensington, the district of London where I was born. We were to meet at South Kensington Station, within walking distance of the museums, also the Albert Hall, Kensington Gardens, the Serpentine, Round Pond etc. He telephoned me in good time and said cheerfully that he would buy an umbrella on the way.

Arrived at our local station, 20 minutes from home, I found it closed. I decided to risk the cost and take a taxi. Luckily I was able to share one with a middle-aged business man. I walked round South Kensington Station, also closed, with no idea of the nature of the disruption. My analyst did not appear. When questioned a London Transport official said: 'The whole network is slightly out of order', or words to that effect. Dismissing an old lady's bravado in asking how to walk home, he simply told me of the No.74 bus.

I was not angry with the bombers but compassionate towards the victims. A day or two later I telephoned our Kosovan muslim friends to remind them of our steady support. Meeting them soon after our son Peter's suicide their occasional company had been a great blessing - here were charming healthy children with congenial parents.

When I asked my analyst about a future date for our Kensington meeting, he said

'The bomb'.

ON WANDSWORTH BRIDGE

Let there be no next episode for me.
I can only stomach scattered moments
Of heaven: like the grey afternoon
On Wandsworth Bridge when I watched the broad sweep
Of tarmac, felt at home with enormous hoardings.
Showing beer, and red and green garage scene,
Looked up with awe at thick dark cylinders
Of coopers plant, observed dun pavement, mustard sky.
Grind of traffic, slap of rain.

On Dying, April 2006

Craving nothing, having all
with daffodils dead,
pear trees in bloom,
I can read of a bloodthirsty march
and still be calm.

My Bible, mug-marked
on the leather cover,
yet holding Isaiah,
the Psalms
and sayings on the Mount,

retains its quality and force.
Each square window opposite
of the high rise flats
is also precious to me
with a bond defying doubt.

My face and hands
are bruised and discoloured –
dying like the GP said.
Anxiety about current loves
no longer makes a ripple.

Sitting quietly
my body feels at ease.
I glimpse familiar faces, yearn for them,
but when I think I may not see
my poems come to print, I weep indeed.

AFTERWORD
MARIEGOLD HERON - 1929 - 2006

A Londoner all her life except for wartime evacuation to Sussex, Mariegold Heron was born Mariegold Proctor in 1929 of a Jewish mother and a Gentile father. The youngest of four children of practising artists, living in comfort in Kensington, she was drawn to poetry by her love of fairy stories.

Brought up in her father's religion, she was all her life a practising, questioning Anglican Christian. But an important influence in her twenties and early thirties was her work in a progressive modern art gallery in Mayfair run by three Jewish partners. An article she wrote describing the gallery and its owners, Roland, Browse and Delbanco, was published in The London Magazine a few years ago.

There has hardly been an Anglo-Jewish element recognized as such among writers in England as there has been a Franco-Semitic element in France (Proust, Montaigne et al). The French writer Gide noted that "the best critics and the best artists are usually to be found among those who have inherited a mixed strain. In them opposing stresses coexist, grow to maturity, and neutralize one another".

Co-existing with these qualities in Mariegold were a sensibility and excitability of temperament, but also the delicate health that might be expected to attend them. Following marriage and the birth of her son, she suffered a breakdown requiring psychiatric care (see

'*Park Gate, South-Western Health Trust*) from which her recovery was a long haul involving psychoanalysis (In *Haycombe Cemetery, Bath - to a psychoanalyst* and Not forgetting the prophet Freud in *Beating Down the Brambles*).

Within a few years she had fought her way back to normal living and motherhood of her then vigorous and intelligent little son.

Before that, Mariegold had laid foundations for her future drive in poetry, with training in voice production, where her awards included one in Bible reading. Her own reading had been very wide, including all of Proust's *A la Recherche du Temps Perdu* where she had noted his genius for illuminating the ordinary.

As well as Mariegold's own delicate health, there had been a shadow over her family background - her mother had suffered depression and her older brother was to become schizophrenic - engaging her attention until he died in middle age. Then her own son developed symptoms of the same illness at the end of his teens until his death at the age of 32. Her responses to this tragedy were active and close, whether he was living at home or in institutional care. For seven years she also worked at a weekly drop-in centre for mental sufferers.

Yet, during this domestically difficult period and in that following her son's death, Mariegold was to pursue the study and practice of poetry with more application and push than she seemed to have had before. Perhaps this was attributable to the long process of psychoanalysis bringing out her Jewish element with increasing focus upon poetry. This included attendance at workshops in London, out in the country and abroad. A collection of her Poems and Prose 1963 - 1991 had been put together and circulated among friends and family, and she gave readings to various groups including The Poetry Society. A number of poems were published in journals and a newspaper (see Acknowledgements).

An academic year was spent studying in Ireland where she gained an MA degree in Creative Writing (Poetry), and a strong affection for that country. She had made visits also to Europe, America and Israel. Still, for her last forty years she occupied the same house, with the same husband, near Wimbledon Common in south London.

With her strong sense of the symbolic factor underlying ordinary actions, Mariegold Heron's poems are deeply felt, closely rooted in her own personal, spiritual and day-to-day life.

Photograph of author in 1964